Questions and Answers About

THE ERIE CANAL

SAMMI JAMESON

NEW YORK

Published in 2019 by The Rosen Publishing Group, Inc.
29 East 21st Street, New York, NY 10010

First Edition

Editor: Elizabeth Krajnik
Book Design: Michael Flynn

Photo Credits: Cover, p. 9 Courtesy of the Library of Congress; cover, pp. 1, 3–26, 28, 30–32 (background texture) NuConcept Dezine/Shutterstock.com; p. 4–5 © North Wind Picture Archives; p. 6 © Collection of the New-York Historical Society, USA/Bridgeman Images; p. 7 from the Internet Archive, https://archive.org/details/cihm_21766; p. 8 Courtesy of eriecanal.org; p. 11 Fotosearch/Archive Photos/Getty Images; p. 12 https://en.wikipedia.org/wiki/Benjamin_Wright#/media/File:Benjamin_Wright.jpg; pp. 13, 15 Courtesy of the New York Public Library; p. 16 Pantheon/SuperStock; p. 17 Robert Asento/Shutterstock.com; pp. 19, 25 Courtesy of the Library of Congress Rare Book and Special Collections Division, Printed Ephemera Collection; pp. 20–21 Interim Archives/Archive Photos/Getty Images; p. 23 Universal History Archive/Universal Images Group/Getty Images; p. 27 SuperStock; p. 29 Bettmann/Getty Images; p. 30 IkeHayden/Shutterstock.com.

Cataloging-in-Publication Data

Names: Jameson, Sammi.
Title: Questions and answers about the Erie Canal / Sammi Jameson.
Description: New York : PowerKids Press, 2019. | Series: Eye on historical sources | Includes glossary and index.
Identifiers: LCCN ISBN 9781538341162 (pbk.) | ISBN 9781538341155 (library bound) | ISBN 9781538341179 (6 pack)
Subjects: LCSH: Erie Canal (N.Y.)–Juvenile literature. | Erie Canal (N.Y.)–History–Juvenile literature.
Classification: LCC HE396.E6 J36 2019 | DDC 386'.48'09747–dc23

Manufactured in the United States of America

CPSIA Compliance Information: Batch #CS18PK: For Further Information contact Rosen Publishing, New York, New York at 1-800-237-9932

CONTENTS

DOUBT LEADS TO INNOVATION 4

HAWLEY'S VISION 6

RAISING SUPPORT AND BUILDING THE CANAL 8

AN ENGINEERING MARVEL 10

FOUR CANAL SURVEYORS 12

OVERCOMING OBSTACLES 14

AQUEDUCT BRIDGES 16

A POPULAR ROUTE 18

ECONOMIC GROWTH 20

THE CANAL AND THE RAILROAD 22

CHANGES TO THE CANAL 24

THE ERIE BARGE CANAL 26

CANAL SONGS 28

THE MODERN CANAL 30

GLOSSARY 31

INDEX 32

WEBSITES 32

DOUBT LEADS TO INNOVATION

In the early 19th century, cross-country travel was hard and took a long time. Traveling to new territories acquired through the Louisiana Purchase in 1803 required crossing the Appalachian Mountains. In 1807, a flour merchant named Jesse Hawley proposed a canal that would connect the Hudson River to Lake Erie, making passage through the Appalachian Mountains far easier.

Sources from the Past

This hand-colored woodcut map showing the areas through which the Erie Canal passed is considered a primary source. Primary sources are original documents created during the time period we're studying. This map is a primary source because it was created when the Erie Canal was in use. Primary sources help us understand history and lead to better study skills. How do you think this map was useful to people in the 1800s?

In 1817, DeWitt Clinton, the governor of New York, convinced the state to spend $7 million on the Erie Canal project. Many people didn't agree with his decision, calling the project "Clinton's Folly" or "Clinton's Ditch." However, when the project was completed in 1825, it was an almost instant success. As a result of the project, **innovative** new **technologies** were introduced which helped boost the economies of cities and towns across New York.

TODAY, THE ERIE CANAL ISN'T AS IMPORTANT TO THE U.S. ECONOMY AS IT WAS IN THE 19TH AND 20TH CENTURIES. HOWEVER, IT'S STILL AN ICONIC PART OF U.S. HISTORY. MANY PEOPLE CONTINUE TO VISIT IT TO LEARN ABOUT ITS HISTORY.

MAP OF THE ERIE CANAL (1800s)

HAWLEY'S VISION

Jesse Hawley's vision came true after he fell on hard times. As a flour merchant, he had to move his goods from place to place by wagon. This cost him—and other merchants—a lot of money.

Hawley studied maps for several months before he figured out a way to connect the Hudson River to Lake Erie. This would help merchants like him move their goods across the Appalachian Mountains faster and for less money. From there, the goods could be shipped throughout the rest of the United States.

DEWITT CLINTON

Hawley published essays, or short pieces of writing, about his idea in the *Genesee Messenger* in 1807 and 1808. DeWitt Clinton, who was a senator at the time, read these essays in the newspaper and decided Hawley's idea was good.

AN ESSAY

ON THE

ENLARGEMENT

OF THE

ERIE CANAL,

WITH ARGUMENTS IN FAVOR OF RETAINING THE PRESENT PROPOSED SIZE OF SEVENTY FEET BY SEVEN; AND FOR ITS ENTIRE LENGTH FROM ALBANY TO BUFFALO WITHOUT ANY DIMINUTION.

BY JESSE HAWLEY.

LOCKPORT, N. Y.
PRINTED AT THE COURIER OFFICE.
1840.

HAWLEY WAS INTERESTED IN THE ERIE CANAL LONG AFTER ITS COMPLETION IN 1825. HE WROTE THIS ESSAY IN 1840 AND INCLUDED SUGGESTIONS TO IMPROVE THE CANAL AND MAKE IT LARGER.

Sources from the Past

Do you think Hawley's essays are primary sources? Were they created during the time period of study? Do you think they provide knowledge about what life was like in the 1800s? If you don't think they should be considered primary sources, why do you think that?

RAISING SUPPORT AND BUILDING THE CANAL

Clinton wanted to raise public support for the canal. He did this by writing a letter to the state government and giving speeches. People doubted Clinton's efforts, but he was certain Hawley's plan would work. After Clinton convinced the state to put $7 million aside for the canal's construction, work began in 1817.

Sources from the Past

Charles Yardley Turner created a pair of murals, or large paintings on a wall, for DeWitt Clinton High School in 1905. *Marriage of the Waters* is one of these murals. Do you think this is a primary source? Why or why not?

CHARLES YARDLEY TURNER'S *MARRIAGE OF THE WATERS* SHOWS DEWITT CLINTON POURING WATER FROM LAKE ERIE INTO THE ATLANTIC OCEAN. THIS ACTION **SYMBOLIZED** THE JOINING OF THE TWO BODIES OF WATER BY THE ERIE CANAL.

FIRST BOAT ON THE ERIE CANAL

The Erie Canal was finished in 1825, and a large celebration was held from October 26 to November 4 to mark its completion. Clinton and other well-known New York citizens boarded a canal boat named the *Seneca Chief*, which would travel from Lake Erie to New York Harbor. The trip took nine days. Once the *Seneca Chief* reached New York Harbor, Clinton made a speech and poured water from Lake Erie into the Atlantic Ocean.

AN ENGINEERING MARVEL

When the Erie Canal was built, there were no engineering schools in the United States. Many of the people who helped build the canal had no engineering experience. During construction, they created new machines and devices to help them do their work. These workers became known as the Erie School of Engineers.

Some of the most important machines invented at this time were those that allowed workers to clear areas of land. One brought down a tree without the worker using a saw or an axe. Another pulled tree stumps from the ground. The wheelbarrow was also improved during this time.

The engineers created a system of **locks** that were better than those used in the United States in earlier years. This system of locks allowed boats to travel in both directions on the canal.

THIS IMAGE SHOWS THE PROCESS OF EXCAVATING, OR
DIGGING UP AND REMOVING, THE EARTH TO CREATE THE
ERIE CANAL. THE MEN IN THE IMAGE ARE USING NEW
MACHINES TO LIFT THE DIRT OUT OF THE WAY.

FOUR CANAL SURVEYORS

The canal was divided into three main sections: eastern, middle, and western. Each section presented its own set of challenges. Four men were made surveyors of the canal: Benjamin Wright, James Geddes, Nathan Roberts, and Charles Brodhead. Surveyors measure the size, shape, and boundaries of areas of land. However, none of these men were surveyors by trade. Three practiced law and one was a teacher.

BENJAMIN WRIGHT WAS A JUDGE BY TRADE. HE WAS ALSO A SKILLED AND HONEST SURVEYOR, WHICH IS WHY HE WAS CHOSEN TO BE THE CHIEF ENGINEER ON THE ERIE CANAL.

The surveyors' measurements had to be very precise, or exact. Even though they weren't very experienced, they learned quickly. Wright and Geddes were asked to run levels on the canal course in spring 1818. Each took a different route across New York from Rome to Syracuse, covering a 100-mile (161 km) loop. They then compared their measurements. The difference was less than 2 inches (5 cm).

OVERCOMING OBSTACLES

One of the greatest obstacles, or challenges, the Erie Canal engineers faced was a steep rock cliff near Niagara Falls in Western New York. To reach Lake Erie, the engineers needed to find a way to get boats up and over the 70-foot (21 m) ridge. Nathan Roberts, an assistant engineer on the Erie Canal, was put to the task.

Roberts knew it wouldn't be possible to reach the top of the ridge with a single pair of locks. He created a series of five double locks that looked like a giant flight of stairs. This was the first time a series of locks this **complex** had been created. The locks became known as the Flight of Five. In 1918, a flight of two locks took the place of the locks on the westbound side.

LOCKPORT IS THE TOWN IN WESTERN NEW YORK IN WHICH THE FLIGHT OF FIVE IS LOCATED. THIS IMAGE SHOWS THE VIEW LOOKING EAST FROM THE TOP OF ONE OF THE LOCKS.

Sources from the Past

This print by William Tombleson is based on an illustration by William H. Bartlett from 1839. Which one do you think is considered the primary source? Why do you think so?

AQUEDUCT BRIDGES

Another obstacle the engineers of the Erie Canal had to overcome was how to get across rivers and creeks. The answer they came up with was to build an **aqueduct** bridge. An aqueduct bridge had to be wide enough for the canal itself and for the towpath alongside it. Canal boats didn't have engines or sails. Instead, they were towed by teams of horses or mules that walked along the towpath.

ROCHESTER AQUEDUCT AROUND 1900

One of the longest aqueduct bridges of the Erie Canal crosses the Genesee River in Rochester. It was built of stones, all of which were **quarried** and shaped by hand. The aqueduct bridge in Rochester, like the Flight of Five in Lockport, became one of the most amazing accomplishments of the canal.

A POPULAR ROUTE

The Erie Canal was a popular travel route even before it was completed. The section of the Erie Canal between Rome and Utica opened in October 1819. Its success helped fuel canal building in other parts of the northeastern United States. In 1824, the passage of boats on sections of canal that were open allowed the state of New York to collect $300,000 in **tolls**.

After the Erie Canal was completed, it became a popular route for transporting, or carrying, goods. Because boats could carry more freight on the canal than wagons on land could, the cost of transporting goods went down.

Within the first nine years of being open, the Erie Canal had paid for itself. After the costs of construction were covered, the state used funds raised by collecting tolls to build other canals.

TABLE OF THE NEW RATES OF TOLL
ON THE ERIE CANAL,

As established by the Canal board, and in effect on said Canal.

Produce, &c.

Miles	BUFFALO.	Toll of a bbl Flour. (C M F)	100 lbs 4. m. (C M F)	100 lbs 3. m. (C M F)	100 lbs 2. m. (C M F)	100 lbs 1. m. (C M F)
0	BUFFALO.					
3	Black Rock,	0 2 5.9.0	0 1 2	0 0 9	0 0 6	0 0 3
4	LOWER BLACK ROCK,	0 3 4.5.6	0 1 6	0 1 2	0 0 8	0 0 4
12	Tonawanda,	1 0 3.6.8	0 4 8	0 3 6	0 2 4	0 1 2
18	H. Brockway's,	1 3 5.5.2	0 7 2	0 5 4	0 3 6	0 1 8
23	Welch's,	1 9 8.7.2	0 9 2	0 6 9	0 4 6	0 2 3
24	Pendleton,	2 0 7.3.6	0 9 6	0 7 6	0 4 8	0 2 4
31	LOCKPORT,	2 6 7.8.4	1 2 4	0 9 3	0 6 2	0 3 1
37	Orange Port,	3 1 9.6.8	1 4 8	1 1 1	0 7 4	0 3 7
38	Gasport,	3 2 8.3.2	1 5 2	1 1 4	0 7 6	0 3 8
43	Reynold's Basin,	3 4 5.6.0	1 6 0	1 2 0	0 8 0	0 4 0
43	Middleport,	3 7 1.5.2	1 7 2	1 2 9	0 8 6	0 4 3
46	Shelby Basin,	3 9 7.4.4	1 8 4	1 3 8	0 9 2	0 4 6
49	Medina,	4 2 3.3.6	1 9 6	1 4 7	0 9 8	0 4 9
52	Road Culvert,	4 4 9.2.8	2 0 8	1 5 6	1 0 4	0 5 2
55	Knowlesville,	4 5 7.9.2	2 1 2	1 5 9	1 0 6	0 5 3
55	Long Bridge,	4 7 5.2.0	2 2 0	1 6 5	1 1 0	0 5 5
57	Eagle Harbor,	4 9 2.4.8	2 2 8	1 7 1	1 1 4	0 5 7
58	Gaines' Basin,	5 0 1.1.2	2 3 2	1 7 4	1 1 6	0 5 8
60	ALBION,	5 1 8.4.0	2 4 0	1 8 0	1 2 0	0 6 0
64	Hindsburgh,	5 5 2.9.6	2 5 6	1 9 2	1 2 8	0 6 4
66	Hulberton,	5 7 0.2.4	2 6 4	1 9 8	1 3 2	0 6 6
70	Holley,	6 0 4.8.0	2 8 0	2 1 0	1 4 0	0 7 0
75	BROCKPORT,	6 4 *.0.0	3 0 0	2 2 5	1 5 0	0 7 5
77	Cooley's Basin,	6 6 5.2.8	3 0 8	2 3 1	1 5 4	0 7 7
80	Adams' Basin,	6 9 1.2.0	3 2 0	2 4 0	1 6 0	0 8 0
83	Spencer's Basin,	7 1 7.1.2	3 3 2	2 4 9	1 6 6	0 8 3
85	Brockway's,	7 3 4.4.0	3 4 0	2 5 5	1 7 0	0 8 5
99	ROCHESTER,	8 2 0.8.0	3 8 0	2 8 5	1 9 0	0 9 5
99	Lock No. 3,	8 5 5.3.6	3 9 6	2 9 7	1 9 8	0 9 9
101	Billinghast's Basin,	8 7 2.6.4	4 0 4	3 0 3	2 0 2	1 0 1
105	Pittsford,	9 0 7.2.0	4 2 0	3 1 5	2 1 0	1 0 5
108	Bushnell's Basin,	9 3 3.1.2	4 3 2	3 2 4	2 1 6	1 0 8
111	Fullam's Basin,	9 5 9.0.4	4 4 4	3 3 3	2 2 2	1 1 1
112	Fairport,	9 6 7.6.8	4 4 8	3 3 6	2 2 4	1 1 2
113	Perrinton centre,	9 7 6 3.2	4 5 2	3 3 9	2 2 6	1 1 3
115	Perrinton,	9 9 3.6.0	4 6 0	3 4 5	2 3 0	1 1 5
117	Wayneport,	1 0 1 0.8.8	4 6 8	3 5 1	2 3 4	1 1 7
120	Macedonville,	1 0 3 6.8.0	4 8 0	3 6 0	2 4 0	1 2 0
123	PALMYRA,	1 0 7 1.3.6	4 9 6	3 7 2	2 4 8	1 2 4
129	Port Gibson,	1 1 1 4.5.6	5 1 6	3 8 7	2 5 8	1 2 9
132	Newark,	1 1 4 0.4.8	5 2 8	3 9 6	2 6 4	1 3 2
133	Lockville,	1 1 4 9.1.2	5 3 2	3 9 9	2 6 6	1 3 3
139	LYONS,	1 2 0 0.9.6	5 5 6	4 1 7	2 7 8	1 3 9
142	Lock Berlin,	1 2 3 5.5.2	5 7 2	4 2 9	2 8 6	1 4 3
148	Clyde,	1 2 7 4.7.2	5 9 2	4 4 4	2 9 6	1 4 8
153	Lockpit,	1 3 2 1.9.2	6 1 2	4 5 9	3 0 6	1 5 3
159	MONTEZUMA,	1 3 7 3.7.6	6 3 6	4 7 7	3 1 8	1 5 9
165	Port Byron,	1 4 2 5.6.0	6 6 0	4 9 5	3 3 0	1 6 5
167	Centreport,	1 4 4 2.8.8	6 6 8	5 0 1	3 3 4	1 6 7
168	Weedsport,	1 4 5 1.5.2	6 7 2	5 0 4	3 3 6	1 6 8
173	Cold Spring,	1 4 9 4.7.2	6 9 2	5 1 9	3 4 6	1 7 3
174	Jordan,	1 5 0 3.3.6	6 9 6	5 2 2	3 4 8	1 7 4
178	Peru,	1 5 3 7.9.2	7 1 2	5 3 4	3 5 6	1 7 8
180	Canton,	1 5 5 5.2.0	7 2 0	5 4 0	3 6 0	1 8 0
185	Camillus,	1 5 9 8.4.0	7 4 0	5 5 5	3 7 0	1 8 5
186	Nine Mile Creek,	1 6 0 7.0.4	7 4 4	5 5 8	3 7 2	1 8 6
187	Bellisle,	1 6 1 5.6.5	7 4 8	5 6 1	3 7 4	1 8 7
191	Geddes,	1 6 5 0.2.4	7 6 4	5 7 3	3 8 2	1 9 1
193	SYRACUSE,	1 6 6 7.5.2	7 7 2	5 7 9	3 8 6	1 9 3
194	Lodi,	1 6 7 6.1.6	7 7 6	5 8 2	3 8 8	1 9 4
199	Orville Feeder,	1 7 1 9.3.6	7 9 6	5 9 7	3 9 8	1 9 9
201	Limestone Feeder,	1 7 3 6.6.4	8 0 4	6 0 3	4 0 2	2 0 1
202	Manlius,	1 7 4 5.2.8	8 0 8	6 0 6	4 0 4	2 0 2
204	Little Lake,	1 7 6 2.5.6	8 1 6	6 1 2	4 0 8	2 0 4
206	Kirkville,	1 7 7 9.8.4	8 2 4	6 1 8	4 1 2	2 0 6
208	Pool's Brook,	1 7 9 7.1.2	8 3 2	6 2 4	4 1 6	2 0 8
211	Chittenango,	1 8 2 3.0.4	8 4 4	6 3 3	4 2 2	2 1 1
214	New Boston,	1 8 4 8.9.6	8 5 6	6 4 2	4 2 8	2 1 4
218	Canastota,	1 8 8 3.5.2	8 7 2	6 5 4	4 3 6	2 1 8
222	Oneida Creek,	1 9 1 8.0.8	8 8 8	6 6 6	4 4 4	2 2 2
226	Loomis,	1 9 5 2.6.4	9 0 4	6 7 8	4 5 2	2 2 6
228	Higgins',	1 9 6 9.9.2	9 1 2	6 8 4	4 5 6	2 2 8
232	New London,	2 0 0 4.4.8	9 2 8	6 9 6	4 6 4	2 3 2
234	Stony Creek,	2 0 2 1.7.6	9 3 6	7 0 2	4 6 8	2 3 4
235	Hawley's Basin,	2 0 3 0.4.0	9 4 0	7 0 5	4 7 0	2 3 5
237	Wood Cr'k Aqueduct,	2 0 4 7.6.8	9 4 8	7 1 1	4 7 4	2 3 7
239	ROME,	2 0 6 4.9.6	9 5 6	7 1 7	4 7 8	2 3 9
247	Oriskany,	2 1 3 4.0.8	9 8 8	7 4 1	4 9 4	2 4 7
250	Whitesboro',	2 1 6 0.0.0	1 0 0 0	7 5 0	5 0 0	2 5 0
251	York Mills,	2 1 6 8.6.4	1 0 0 4	7 5 3	5 0 2	2 5 1
254	UTICA,	2 1 9 4.5.6	1 0 1 6	7 6 2	5 0 8	2 5 4
257	Ferguson's,	2 2 2 0.4.8	1 0 2 8	7 7 1	5 1 4	2 5 7

Merchandize Furn't.

Miles	ALBANY.	100 lbs 3. m. (C M F)	100 lbs 5. m. (C M F)	100 lbs 3. m. (C M F)
0	ALBANY.			
5	Port Schuyler,	0 4 0	0 2 5	0 1 5
6	Gibbonsville,	0 4 8	0 3 0	0 1 8
7	WEST TROY,	0 5 6	0 3 5	0 2 1
10	Cohoes,	0 8 0	0 5 0	0 3 0
13	Lower Aqueduct,	1 0 4	0 6 5	0 3 9
19	Willow Spring,	1 5 2	0 9 5	0 5 7
26	Upper Aqueduct,	2 0 8	1 3 0	0 7 8
30	SCHENECTADY,	2 4 0	1 5 0	0 9 0
39	Rotterdam,	3 1 2	1 9 5	1 1 7
44	Phillip's Locks,	3 5 2	2 2 0	1 3 2
45	Florida,	3 6 0	2 2 5	1 3 5
47	Amsterdam, [Port Jackson.]	3 7 6	2 3 5	1 4 1
52	Schoharie Creek,	4 1 6	2 6 0	1 5 6
54	Smithtown,	4 3 2	2 7 0	1 6 2
57	FULTONVILLE,	4 5 6	2 8 5	1 7 1
64	Big Nose,	5 1 2	3 2 0	1 9 2
66	Spraker's Basin,	5 2 8	3 3 0	1 9 8
69	Canajoharie,	5 5 2	3 4 5	2 0 7
72	Fort Plain,	5 7 6	3 6 0	2 1 6
75	Diefendorf's Land'g	6 0 0	3 7 5	2 2 5
77	St. Johnsville,	6 1 6	3 8 5	2 3 1
81	East Canada Creek,	6 4 8	4 0 5	2 4 3
83	Indian Castle, [Newandaga Creek.]	6 6 4	4 1 5	2 4 9
86	Fink's Ferry,	6 8 8	4 3 0	2 5 8
88	LITTLE FALLS,	7 0 4	4 4 0	2 6 4
91	Rankin's L'k No. 7,	7 2 8	4 5 5	2 7 3
95	Herkimer lo'r br'ge,	7 6 0	4 7 5	2 8 5
96	Mohawk,	7 6 8	4 8 0	2 8 8
97	Fulmer's Creek,	7 7 6	4 8 5	2 9 1
98	Morgan's Landing,	7 8 4	4 9 0	2 9 4
99	Steele's Creek,	7 9 2	4 9 5	2 9 7
101	Frankfort,	8 0 8	5 0 5	3 0 3
107	Ferguson's,	8 5 6	5 3 5	3 2 1
110	UTICA,	8 8 0	5 5 0	3 3 0
113	York Mills,	9 0 4	5 6 5	3 3 9
114	Whitesboro',	9 1 2	5 7 0	3 4 2
117	Oriskany,	9 3 6	5 8 5	3 5 1
125	ROME,	1 0 0 0	6 2 5	3 7 5
127	Wood C'k Aqueduct [Fort Ball.]	1 0 1 6	6 3 5	3 8 1
129	Hawley's Basin,	1 0 3 2	6 4 5	3 8 7
130	Stony Creek,	1 0 4 0	6 5 0	3 9 0
138	New London,	1 0 5 6	6 6 0	3 9 6
135	Higgins',	1 0 8 8	6 8 0	4 0 8
138	Loomis',	1 1 0 4	6 9 0	4 1 4
141	Oneida Creek, [Durhamville.]	1 1 2 8	7 0 5	4 2 3
146	Canastota,	1 1 6 8	7 3 0	4 3 8
150	New Boston,	1 2 0 0	7 5 0	4 5 0
153	Chittenango,	1 2 2 4	7 6 5	4 5 9
156	Pool's Brook,	1 2 4 8	7 8 0	4 6 8
158	Kirkville,	1 2 6 4	7 9 0	4 7 4
160	Little Lake,	1 2 8 0	8 0 0	4 8 0
162	Manlius,	1 2 9 6	8 1 0	4 8 6
163	Limestone Feeder, [Hall's Landing.]	1 3 0 4	8 1 5	4 8 9
165	Orville Feeder,	1 3 2 0	8 2 5	4 9 5
170	Lodi,	1 3 6 0	8 5 0	5 1 0
171	SYRACUSE,	1 3 6 8	8 5 5	5 1 3
173	Geddes,	1 3 8 4	8 6 5	5 1 9
177	Bellisle,	1 4 1 6	8 8 5	5 3 1
178	Nine Mile Creek,	1 4 2 4	8 9 0	5 3 4
179	Camillus,	1 4 3 2	8 9 5	5 3 7
184	Canton,	1 4 7 2	9 2 0	5 5 2
186	Peru,	1 4 8 8	9 3 0	5 5 8
190	Jordan,	1 5 2 0	9 5 0	5 7 0
191	Cold Spring,	1 5 2 8	9 5 5	5 7 3
196	Weedsport,	1 5 6 8	9 6 0	5 8 8
197	Centreport,	1 5 7 6	9 8 5	5 9 1
199	Port Byron,	1 5 9 2	9 9 5	5 9 7
205	MONTEZUMA,	1 6 4 0	1 0 2 5	6 1 5
211	Lockpit,	1 6 8 8	1 0 5 5	6 3 3
216	Clyde,	1 7 2 8	1 0 8 0	6 4 8
221	Lock Berlin,	1 7 6 8	1 1 0 5	6 6 3
225	LYONS,	1 8 0 0	1 1 2 5	6 7 5
231	Lockville,	1 8 4 8	1 1 5 5	6 9 3
232	Newark,	1 8 5 6	1 1 6 0	6 9 6
235	Port G bson,	1 8 8 0	1 1 7 5	7 0 5
240	PALMYRA,	1 9 2 0	1 2 0 0	7 2 0
244	Macedonville,	1 9 5 2	1 2 2 0	7 3 2
247	Wayneport,	1 9 7 6	1 2 3 5	7 4 1
249	Perrinton,	1 9 9 2	1 2 4 5	7 4 7
251	Perrinton Centre,	2 0 0 8	1 2 5 5	7 5 3
252	Fairport,	2 0 1 6	1 2 6 0	7 5 6

Sources from the Past

This table shows the toll rates on different kinds of freight. Tables such as these are considered primary sources. Toll rates tell us important information about the time period of study. Today, the value of money is different. We don't use mills, or one-tenth of a cent, anymore. However, this form of money was used when the Erie Canal was still operating.

ECONOMIC GROWTH

The Erie Canal's success directly affected the communities surrounding it. The populations of cities such as Utica, Syracuse, and Buffalo increased in about 20 years. Recognizing the canal's importance to the state's economy, the New York State government decided to make the canal larger so it could handle bigger boats carrying more freight.

Work on the canal had to be stopped when the **Depression** of 1837 hit, but it started again in 1853. By 1860, **commerce** on the canal had increased greatly. In 1862, the canal enlargement project was completed and the state collected more than $4.5 million in tolls.

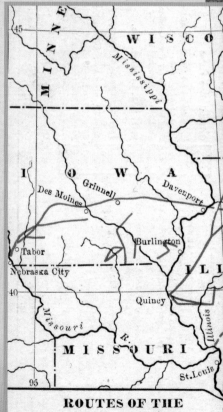

ROUTES OF THE
UNDERGROUND
RAILROAD
1830 - 1865

The canal was very important in shaping the growth of cities and economies throughout much of the nation. It linked northeastern states to the Midwest economically, socially, and politically by transporting goods as well as settlers.

THE ERIE CANAL SERVED AN IMPORTANT ROLE IN THE UNDERGROUND RAILROAD, A SYSTEM OF PEOPLE WHO HELPED RUNAWAY SLAVES FROM THE SOUTH ESCAPE TO THE NORTH AND CANADA.

ERIE CANAL

THE CANAL AND THE RAILROAD

The first railroad in New York State opened in 1831, stretching 16 miles (25.7 km) from Albany to Schenectady. This line operated together with **packet boats** to Utica, Rochester, and Buffalo. By taking the train instead of the canal, travelers shortened their journey by one day.

Soon, however, the railroads began to compete with the Erie Canal. The Utica and Schenectady Railroad, which ran alongside the Erie Canal, was completed in 1836, making it possible to travel and transport goods from Albany to Utica by train.

The New York State government was afraid the railroad would take business away from the canal and thus put a law in place making it illegal for trains to carry freight. However, by the 1850s, the government allowed the Utica and Schenectady Railroad to carry freight.

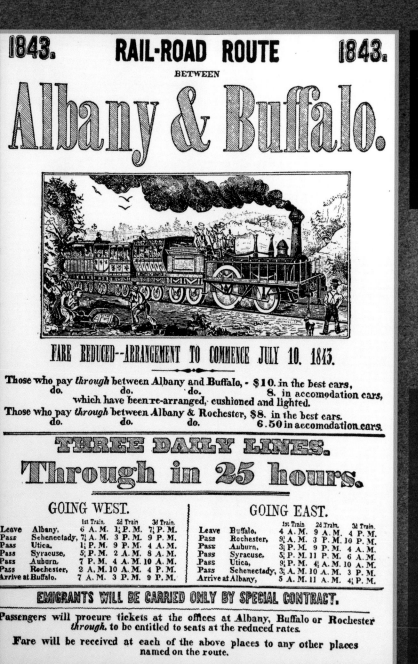

OVER TIME, RAILROADS BECAME MORE POPULAR BECAUSE THEY COULD FOLLOW ROUTES THAT WERE BEYOND THE REACH OF THE CANAL. THEY ALSO OFFERED A MORE LUXURIOUS RIDE THAN CANAL BOATS, AND THEY COULD TRANSPORT GOODS AND PEOPLE FASTER.

Sources from the Past

This poster for the Albany and Buffalo Railroad from 1843 advertises reduced ticket fare choices. Railroads competed with the canal because they were a cheaper and quicker way to travel. This poster is a primary source. Is there any additional information we can gather from this poster?

CHANGES TO THE CANAL

To compete with the railroads, changes to the canal had to be made. In 1882, New York State did away with the tolls to reduce the cost of transporting freight on the canal. People also talked about enlarging the canal again, but some people didn't agree with this idea.

On December 29, 1885, a public meeting was held in New York City. Orlando Brunson Potter, a wealthy New Yorker, spoke in favor of enlarging the canal again. He was certain the railroad wouldn't steal the canal's business and said the enlargement of the canal would benefit farmers, not hurt them.

In 1895, the state approved $9 million for the enlargement of the Erie Canal. However, during the time between the meeting and the approval of the enlargement, the canal lost even more business to the railroad.

IMPORTANCE OF IMPROVING AND MAINTAINING THE ERIE CANAL BY THE STATE OF NEW YORK WITHOUT AID FROM THE GENERAL GOVERNMENT.

ADDRESS

OF

O. B. POTTER

AT A

PUBLIC MEETING HELD IN NEW YORK CITY,

DECEMBER 29, 1885.

FELLOW-CITIZENS :

I am glad to be present with you at this meeting. It is time we commenced the work resolved upon at the Utica conference, of lengthening the locks and deepening the Erie Canal, and putting it in a thorough state of efficiency. This canal has done more for the growth, development and prosperity of the State of New York, and especially of the city of New York, since its construction, than any other agency. If kept free, and in a state of efficiency, it will continue its work of beneficence and blessing to our State for generations. This canal is the only reliable security which the people of this State and of this great city and of our neighboring city of Brooklyn have that the vast commerce of the Mississippi Valley and of the Great Lakes shall continue to come in increasing measure to the port of New York, and through it to the outside world, at rates of freight which will enable New York State and this port and city to maintain their own place in the commerce of this continent and of the world. The line of the Erie Canal, with the Great Lakes, is the natural highway of commerce from the great valley of the Mississippi to the seaboard. It was given to this State by the munificent hand of the Creator for our development and use. If we are true to ourselves, it will continue to be the great highway of commerce from East to West upon this continent in the future as it has been in the past. I know it is said that the railways have superseded, and will supersede, the canal. I deny this proposition ; and maintain that however useful and important the railways (and no man holds their agency in advancing civilization in higher estimate than I do), they by no means supersede the necessity for the maintenance of our canal. The canal developed and called into being the great commerce by which our railways are now largely sup-

THE ERIE BARGE CANAL

After the canal enlargement was approved, very little work was done between 1898 and 1903 because the project became too costly. In 1903, the New York State government passed the **Barge** Canal Act and approved borrowing money to build the Erie Barge Canal. This new canal would combine parts of the Erie Canal with new routes. The barge canal would also be much wider and deeper than the old canal, enabling it to handle much larger boats.

When the canal was enlarged, the towpaths for horses alongside the canal were removed. This meant packet boats could no longer be used. Instead, tugboats towed larger barges and freighters.

The enlargement allowed for larger boats to go through the canal, but the number of boats traveling on the canal continued to decrease. However, the barge canal continued to carry freight for many more years.

THE ERIE BARGE CANAL WAS COMPLETED IN 1918. IT'S 339 MILES (545.6 KM) LONG AND RUNS ACROSS NEW YORK STATE FROM WATERFORD, NEAR ALBANY, TO THE NIAGARA RIVER, NEAR BUFFALO.

CANAL SONGS

Throughout its history, the Erie Canal has held an important place in people's lives and memories. Building and enlarging the canal was hard work. To pass the time, workers would make up songs. Canal boatmen also made up songs about the canal based on songs about the sea.

Some of the people who helped build the Erie Canal came to live in the United States from Ireland. They created the song "Paddy on the Canal" to explain their experience constructing the canal.

The "Erie Canal Song" is a popular folk song. Written by Thomas S. Allen in 1905 and originally titled "Low Bridge, Everybody Down," the title and words of the song have been changed a number of times over the years. Famous musicians, such as Bruce Springsteen, have played the "Erie Canal Song" in front of crowds of people.

"THE MEETING OF THE WATERS/ODE FOR THE CANAL CELEBRATION" IS A SONG WRITTEN FOR THE OPENING DAY OF THE CANAL ON OCTOBER 26, 1825.

OPENING OF THE ERIE CANAL (1825)

THE MODERN CANAL

The high number of boats traveling on the Erie Canal continued until six years after the end of World War II. From then, the number of boats traveling on the canal for trading purposes started to decrease. In 1992, the New York State government created the New York State Canal Corporation to take care of the canal. Commercial traffic on the Erie Canal stopped completely in 1994. In 1996, the Canal Corporation approved a $32 million plan to improve the canal for **recreational** purposes.

In 2000, U.S. Congress established the Erie Canalway National Heritage Corridor to keep the history of the Erie Canal alive. People can bike and walk along special trails and take in the beautiful scenery. In the summer months, towns throughout New York celebrate the canal and all the success and wealth it brought to the state's economy.

GLOSSARY

aqueduct: A man-made channel constructed to move water from one place to another.

barge: A large boat that has a flat bottom and is used to carry goods in harbors and on rivers and canals.

commerce: The large-scale buying and selling of goods and services.

complex: Not easy to understand or explain; having many parts.

depression: A period of time in which there is little economic activity and many people don't have jobs.

innovative: Using or showing new methods or ideas.

lock: A device for raising and lowering ships between stretches of water that are different levels.

packet boat: A boat used to carry mail, freight, or people.

quarry: To dig or take stones from an area of ground, or the area where people dig for stone for building.

recreational: Done for enjoyment.

symbolize: To serve as a representation of something else.

technology: The way people do something and the tools they use.

toll: Money someone is required to pay for the use of a road, bridge, or other route.

INDEX

A

Albany, 22, 23, 27
Appalachian Mountains, 4, 6
aqueduct bridges, 16, 17

B

Brodhead, Charles, 12
Buffalo, 20, 22, 23, 27

C

Clinton, DeWitt, 5, 6, 7, 8, 9

E

Erie Barge Canal, 26, 27
Erie Canalway National Heritage Corridor, 30
Erie School of Engineers, 10

F

freight, 18, 19, 20, 22, 24, 26

G

Geddes, James, 12, 13

H

Hawley, Jesse, 4, 6, 7, 8
Hudson River, 4, 6

L

Lake Erie, 4, 6, 8, 9, 14
Lockport, 14, 15, 17
locks, 10, 14, 15

N

New York State Canal Corporation, 30
Niagara Falls, 14

P

packet boats, 22, 26
Potter, Orlando Brunson, 24, 25

R

railroads, 22, 23, 24
Roberts, Nathan, 12, 14
Rochester, 16, 17, 22
Rome, 13, 18

S

songs, 28, 29
surveyors, 12, 13
Syracuse, 13, 20

T

tolls, 18, 19, 20, 24
towpaths, 16, 26
Turner, Charles Yardley, 8

U

Underground Railroad, 20, 21
Utica, 18, 20, 22

W

Wright, Benjamin, 12, 13

WEBSITES

Due to the changing nature of Internet links, PowerKids Press has developed an online list of websites related to the subject of this book. This site is updated regularly. Please use this link to access the list: www.powerkidslinks.com/eohs/erie